19.9.14

Pie Corbett

SPEAK OUT!

Great ideas for speaking and listening activities for ages 7-9

Illustrations by Helen James

A&C Black • London

First published in 2006 by
A & C Black Publishers Ltd
38 Soho Square, London WID 3HB

www.acblack.com

Text copyright © 2006 Pie Corbett

Designed and illustrated by Helen James
Edited by Mary-Jane Wilkins

ISBN   Hardback 9-780-7136-7220-6
         Paperback 9-780-7136-7221-3

A CIP record for this book is available from
the British Library.

A & C Black uses paper produced with elemental
chlorine-free pulp, harvested from managed
sustainable forests.

Printed in Great Britain by CPD Wales.

Contents

1
Chitter chatter

Everyone loves to talk – in all sorts of different ways.

whinge bawl

babble burble

coo

talk

chatter whisper

gossip

broadcast inform

announce

instruct

chat

tell stories

help

comfort

157 + 14   157 +
             14
             17

interest

speak

inspire

sing

natter

mumble

waffle

discuss

persuade

moan

comment

5

Who do we talk to?

How we talk depends on a number of different things. First of all, it matters who we are talking to. When you talk to different people, you may change what you say and how you speak.

Speak up lad!

talking to other kids

It was well good!

talking to someone with a hearing aid

Yeah Mum...

Do you have the Beano?

talking to a shop assistant

talking on a mobile phone

If we are with our friends we use our own way of talking. In school or other more formal situations – and when talking to adults – we may use different, more formal language. When we talk to strangers, we tend to become more formal.

Who do you find easy to talk to? Find a piece of paper and list the people below in two columns.

Easy to talk to and **Hard to talk to**

Think about how you would change the way you speak for each person.

- teacher
- shopkeeper
- policeman
- friend's mum
- teenager
- lollipop person
- waiter in restaurant
- bus driver
- toddler
- dog
- brother
- doctor
- uncle

I can't hear what you're saying.

teacher

What do we talk about?

The subjects we talk about also change how we speak and listen. If we find a subject interesting, then we may have lots to say and be prepared to listen carefully. If we know a lot about a topic we may find that we have more to say than people who know less about it.

But if we find a topic boring, or we do not know much about it, then we might be fairly quiet and perhaps not even listen very well.

When do we speak and listen well?

We speak and listen well when the subject:
- is interesting,
- is a hobby,
- is something we know lots about already,
- matters,
- will be helpful to us,
- is one we need to know about,
- will get a job done,
- is unusual,
- is funny,
- is exciting.

What sorts of things do you find it interesting to talk about? On a piece of paper write two headings and sort the topics listed below into into two columns.

Easy to talk about   and   **Hard to talk about**

- a favourite TV programme
- clothes
- aliens
- celebrities
- politics
- cars
- space
- pollution

- fishing
- football
- dinosaurs
- golf
- computer games
- pop music
- pets
- clothes

How do these subjects change the way you speak and listen?

How do we talk?

When you want other people to listen to you, remember the following things.

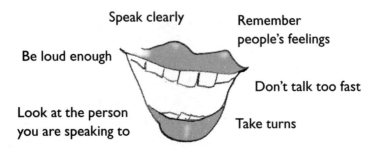

Speak clearly

Remember people's feelings

Be loud enough

Don't talk too fast

Look at the person you are speaking to

Take turns

Have interesting ideas

If you want to be a good listener, then remember to do these things.

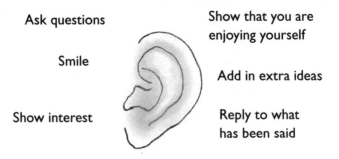

Look at the person speaking

Ask questions

Show that you are enjoying yourself

Smile

Add in extra ideas

Show interest

Reply to what has been said

Try to remember what people have said

Making up class rules

When everyone calls out and talks
at once you can't have a discussion!

In a group, discuss the rules for talking listed below.
Which do you think matters most? Which matters
least? Are there any you could miss out?

Find a piece of paper and write down these rules for
talking in order from 1 to 10. Start with the rule that
you think is most important, and finish with the one
you think is least important. Are there any other class
rules for talking you would like to add? You could turn
your list into a poster for class display.

Talking rules!

- Try to think of new ideas if you are getting stuck.
- Speak clearly so everyone can hear.
- Try to make interesting points.
- Clean your teeth daily.
- Add to other people's ideas.
- Take turns.
- Try to add more points.
- Give reasons for your ideas.
- Don't say nasty things.
- Put your hand up before you speak.

Now here are some rules for good listening. In your group, discuss these too. Which matters most and which least? Are there any you could miss out?

Find another piece of paper and put them in order from 1 to 10. Again, start with the rule that you think is most important and end with the one you think is least important. Can you think of any other listening rules to add? Turn your list into a poster and display it alongside the rules for talking.

Rules for listening

- Remember the main points.
- Wait your turn to speak.
- Don't look out of the window.
- Ask questions.
- Listen to what is being said rather than thinking about what you want to say.
- Keep your ears clean of wax.
- Show you are interested in the speaker.
- Don't interrupt.
- Don't giggle, fidget or whisper while someone is speaking.
- Look at the person who is speaking.

2
Giving a talk

There are lots of times when you might give a talk at school.

Explaining how to do something

Explaining how something works

News time

Telling the class what you have found out

Show and tell

Giving instructions

Evaluating what you have done

How to start

Some people love talking. They natter all the time. But this does not mean that they can stand up in front of the class – or even the whole school – and give a talk. You may get stressed out about the idea of talking in front of people, but a little bit of preparation can help.

Who are you talking to?

The first thing to think about is
– who is your audience?

You need to make sure that they:
• are interested,
• can hear and see.
It's no good droning on in a boring way -- you need
to think about what is interesting about your subject
– and how to speak about it in an interesting manner.

What is your purpose?
What are you trying to do in your talk?
Are you:
• instructing,
• explaining,
• informing,
• persuading,
• reporting?

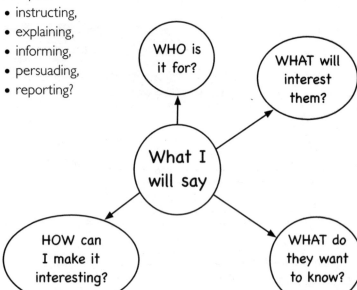

Getting ready

Once you have thought about who you are going to be talking to and what they will want to know, you can set about getting ready.

It's not a good idea just to stand up and talk
– anything could happen:
- you might run out of things to say,
- you could start talking about the wrong things,
- you may forget important things,
- you'll probably repeat yourself.

Your audience will lose interest.

So – get ready properly!
- First of all you need to gather your information,
- Then you need to organize the information into a sensible order,
- Next think of ways of making it memorable,
- Finally, practise your talk before you stand up.

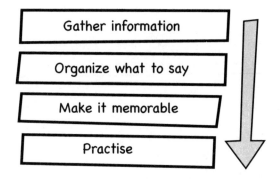

Gather information

Organize what to say

Make it memorable

Practise

Gathering information

Sometimes you may know what you are going to say and don't need much time to prepare. However, you may need to spend some time finding out about your subject.

You might do this by:

- interviewing people,
- using work from lessons,
- reading information books,
- searching through an encyclopaedia,
- using books from the library,
- carrying out an Internet search,
- using CD-ROMs to find information,
- visiting places or talking to visitors,
- writing to someone with questions or to ask for information.

To help you sort your information, draw up a list with two columns.

In the first column, write down everything you know about the subject already. In the second column write down a list of other things it would be interesting or useful to find out.

Here is some information gathering that Tom has been working on to prepare his talk about his favourite creatures – snakes.

What I know	What I want to find out
Snakes are reptiles	Do snakes lay eggs?
They have no legs	
There are 2500 different varieties	Where do snakes live?
Some snakes are poisonous	What do they eat?
Some snakes suffocate their prey	Main food?
Some people keep snakes as pets	How do they kill prey?

Organizing information

Now Tom needs to organize what he is going to say. He could put the information into boxes, using headings for different parts of the talk – rather like paragraphs. Here is one way of organizing Tom's list.

What are snakes?
Snakes are reptiles

What do they look like?
Have no legs
2,500 varieties

What do they eat?
????

Where do they live?
????

How do they kill prey?
Some suffocate their prey
Some are poisonous

Other information
Some kept as pets
Do they lay eggs?

Timetables

There are several different ways to organize information. Here is one way, a timetable.

Our school trip

8.45	leave school
9.30	arrive at castle
10.30	see dungeons
12.00	have lunch
1.00	climb battlements
2.00	watch film
3.00	return to school

Use timetables or time lines for information that needs to be organized by time – the order in which things happen. This is a good way to organize a recount of an event, something that happened in history or what you did on a school trip. Time lines can also be used to organize a sequence of instructions – what to do first, next … and finally!

Flow charts

Flow charts are useful for putting information into boxes and then organizing it in a sequence.

You can use flow charts for reporting information. They can help you give factual talks about what you know, as well as explanations about how something works or why something happens.

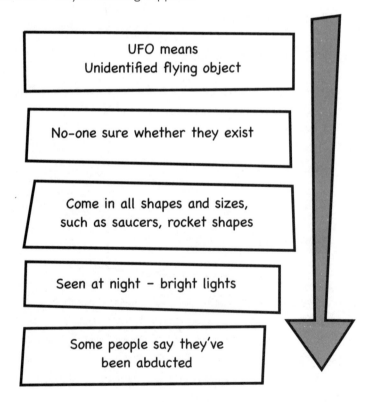

UFO means
Unidentified flying object

No-one sure whether they exist

Come in all shapes and sizes,
such as saucers, rocket shapes

Seen at night – bright lights

Some people say they've
been abducted

Grabbing attention

Most people stand up and say what they want to say and then sit down. Here are some ways to make a talk eye-catching, ear-grabbing and fun!

Eye-catching

Try to think of ways to make your work eye-catching. Can you show any information in pictures? Try to build at least one eye-grabber into your talk, for example, using posters or photographs, the overhead projector, the interactive whiteboard, drawings, diagrams or graphs, objects, video clips, or even objects hidden in a box!

Ear-grabbing

Think of ways to vary the sound of your talk by using different voices or sound effects, music, role play – or even ringing a bell between different sections!

Fun!

Try to think of a few ways to inject some fun or humour into your talk. You could try using jokes, cartoons, role-play, or think of some questions to ask so the talk becomes a bit like a quiz. Try to build in surprising bits of information, scary facts or unusual details.

Keep your talk clear and simple. Don't add too many extras – or you may not put across the facts clearly.

Practice makes perfect

Try to practise giving your talk – especially if you are using extra bits such as role-play or pictures. Here are some important pointers to help you when you are rehearsing.

Volume

Remember that the whole talk will be useless if your audience cannot hear what you are saying. Ask someone to stand at the back of the room and tell you whether they can easily hear what you are saying.

Pace

You don't want to talk slowly, but you need to make sure you don't talk too fast. The key is to be loud and clear and to avoid dashing through what you have to say.

Timing

Find out how long you have to speak for and practise keeping inside the time limit. If you are working in a group, decide who will say which part. Practise so that there are no long pauses between speakers.

Look around

When you are talking, look around at your audience. The talk won't be as effective if you look down to read your words the whole time and don't look at people.

Have a plan

Have a simple plan to follow and make sure you keep to it.

3

Working in a group

Have you ever worked in a group of people who find it hard to get on? Learning how to work together can be easier if you all have some ideas about how to work as a group.

Group roles

Begin by deciding who will take which role in the group. This should not take long. If you work as a group on a regular basis, you may like to take turns in different roles – or you can decide which role suits you best.

Group leader

This person is in charge of running the group and should make sure that everyone keeps to the task and that no one starts talking about other things.

A scribe

This is an important job and is best suited to someone who can take notes quickly. This person writes down the key points that the group agrees upon, ready to feed back to the class. This job should go to someone with reasonable handwriting and spelling.

A reporter

This person feeds back to the rest of the class. The reporter should be someone who is good at speaking loudly and clearly and who can put across what the group decides effectively.

A mentor

The mentor makes sure that everyone has a chance to contribute ideas. It is a good idea for the mentor to go round the group every so often, giving everyone a chance to add more points or suggestions.

A timekeeper

It is so easy to run over time and not complete the task. This member of the group has the job of reminding everyone about the time.

Before you start

Before beginning any group task you need to make sure that you are all clear about the answers to the following questions.

What exactly is the task?

If this is not clear, you are bound to fail. If you do not understand what to do, ask the teacher or group leader. Begin any group task by stating exactly what has to be done. Keep this in mind – it is the group's goal.

How long do you have?

The time keeper has to make sure that the task is completed in time and that no one wastes time.
Try having a '5 minutes to go' signal so you are not caught out by losing track in the last minutes.
Also make sure no one wastes time by wittering on.

What must you achieve?

Make a note at the beginning of exactly what you need to have achieved by the time you finish.

How will you report back?

You may want the group reporter to stand up and feed back your main points. Or using a poster, interactive whiteboard or computer screen may be more effective. Decide at the start how the reporter will feed back.

4

Persuading people

People use talk to persuade other people all the time.

Muuuuuuum, can I have some sweets?

In a newsagent

In the playground

On advertising posters

In TV commercials

27

Persuasive tricks

The best way of finding out how to persuade people is to look at advertisement techniques.

If you watch TV, you will see that the advertisers use all sorts of persuasive tricks to make you want to buy their products. Here are some of their methods.

Pictures can make products look good. Advertisers might show a product in an attractive setting.

Music can add an attractive background.

Sound effects can make products seem to come alive.

Bright colours can make goods seem more exciting.

Celebrities might appear in an ad, which makes people watching think that they can be like the celebrity if they use the product advertised.

Free offers can be tempting, e.g. ads for holidays which say that one child goes free. (This usually means the child sleeping in the same room as the parents!)

Benefits of using a product. Ads using this technique show how using the product might make you healthier, fitter, happier, wealthier, more famous…

Advertisers using talk

How do advertisers use talk to persuade you to rush out and spend all your pocket money on the latest toy? Here are a few techniques.

Questions

Have you noticed how advertisers often use a question to make it seem as though they are talking directly to you? This draws the listener in.

Lists of facts and numbers

Some advertisers support what they are saying by using scientific facts or numbers. This helps to make it sound as though what they are saying is true.

Alliteration

Alliteration occurs when you say words close together that start with the same sound, for example, 'Buy Bill's Burgers'. The effect of the repeated sound makes whatever you are saying more powerful and memorable.

Rhyme

Lots of adverts use rhymes, jingles and songs. These are often set to catchy tunes that stay in your head. If this happens the advertiser has done a good job. The idea is that the tune makes their message memorable.

Powerful words

Nearly all adverts use powerful words – they boast about what they are trying to persuade you to do or buy.

genuine **wonderful**

finest comfortable

ideal *guaranteed*

best

fast

safest

perfect

fantastic **easy**

amazing sensational

genuine **fabulous** coolest

great *softest*

Short, bossy sentences

One other trick advertisers use is to boss the listener. Sentences often start with a verb and sound like an order or command.

Sentences in advertisements are often very short so that the viewer is almost punched by the words.

Avoid disappointment!

Buy now!

Be amazed!

Don't miss!

Don't wait!

See it to believe it!

Grab one now!

Send off for free offer!

Once in a lifetime opportunity!

Repetition

If you listen carefully to some adverts, you will hear the name of the product repeated many times. This is to make sure the listener remembers it. So repeating key points or a message can be very effective way of persuading someone.

Selling a trip into space

Imagine you have been given the task of trying to persuade some people to take a trip into space – maybe to visit a space station on Mars. How would you set about this?

Try to set out clearly what the advantages could be. Make a list of these, as they will be very handy in persuading people to take the trip!

Advantages of taking a trip to Mars
- You'll be the first to make the journey.
- It will be unlike any other trip.
- It may never happen again.
- A once in a lifetime opportunity.
- Not many will have done it.
- Others will be envious of you.
- Amazing sights to see.
- You can sell your story afterwards.

Now think about which talk techniques you could use to persuade people to buy this trip of a lifetime.

Questions
Try speaking directly to the people you want to persuade by using a question and the word 'you'. Make them think about how amazing such a trip would be and how it would make their lives more interesting.

Have you ever felt bored?
Why not take a trip to Mars?

Ever wondered about life in space?
Now you too can experience it.

Want to be the first in your town
to travel to Mars? Read on...

Alliteration

Build some alliteration into your main message.

Make Mars memorable – visit now!

Rhyme

See if you can invent a catchy jingle:

Tired of cars?
Then visit Mars!

Powerful words and short sentences

Dress up the trip so it sounds wonderful: boasting to persuade the listener that the trip will be fantastic. Use short, bossy sentences so that it sounds as if you are instructing the listener to do what you want them to do.

Take the trip of a lifetime to
the most amazing place in space.
See spectacular landscapes.
Marvel at the Earth seen from space.
Travel in luxury at fantastic prices.

Dress it up

You may want to add a few special points to dress up the offer – these are ideas which will make the trip sound even more amazing.

Free offer for the first 50 replies!
Fantastic prices!
Prices lower than last year!
Bargains for all!
Pay later!
Order now for cheap deal!
Free travel bag for all children!

More ideas for adverts

Try out some of your persuasive techniques by pretending to be advertisers. Create a one-minute advertisement to persuade people to do one of the folllowing.

- Travel to the end of the rainbow.
- Visit the three bears' house.
- Take the job of guarding the troll's bridge.
- Not walk through the forest.
- Go to the palace ball.
- Buy a gingerbread man.

Holding a class discussion

Try holding a class discussion to find out
how to persuade people to different views.

Imagine you are going to discuss whether crisps should be
on sale during break time. Split the class in half. One side
prepares reasons for selling crisps at break time in school using
the connectives in the box below. They need to practise what
they will say – writing it down and saying it aloud. For example:

> **We believe that many children would benefit
> from the chance to buy crisps...**

Then give a reason:

> **...because this would give them an energy boost.**

Connectives

We believe...
Our first reason is...
Another reason for saying this...
Furthermore...
Also...
...because...
It is true that...
The main reason to vote for us is that...
Finally...

The other side, who are against selling crisps at break time, needs to make a list of all the reasons it would not be a good idea to do this. They can use the connectives from the box below to practise making points to argue back.

Some people could be in role, acting the part of a parent, a doctor, the owner of a crisp factory or a local shop, or a government health adviser. Think about the views these people might have and which side they should join.

Connectives for responding

On the other hand...
Other people suggest that...
Alternatively...
However...
A different view is to suggest that...
If...
It is not right to say... because...
The other team is incorrect to suggest... because...
We disagree with the view that... because...
Finally, the most important reason you should vote for us is...

Starting and ending the discussion

Someone should begin the discussion by explaining the subject that you are talking about:

We are discussing whether or not...

You can end the discussion with everyone deciding what they think. They should give a reason for what they think, using the word 'because'.

I think that crisps should not be on sale because...

More ideas for class discussions

Here are some more suggestions for discussions.

- Should footballs be banned at playtimes?
- Should fox hunting be banned?
- Should sweets be allowed in school?
- Should children be allowed to choose what they eat at lunchtime?
- Should the school day be longer?
- Should young children have homework?
- Should everyone have to wear school uniform?

5

Newsmakers

We are all curious about other people and how the world works. Becoming a journalist and interviewing other people can help you find information and hear other people's viewpoints.

You might find out:
- facts,
- information about how things work,
- why things don't work,
- reasons why things happen,
- people's experiences,
- what happened in the past,
- people's ideas about what has happened,
- people's ideas about what needs to be done.

Interviewing people is a great way to add more information, views and ideas to any work that you are doing in class. But successful interviews take some preparation and thought. Interviewing is not an easy skill to learn.

Interview skills

Asking people questions sounds quite straightforward, but you need to prepare before you start.

Interviewers should have some way of easily recording what people say. You could work in pairs with one person asking questions and the other writing down answers – this takes quite a time unless you are a very fast writer. Or you could use a tape recorder to record what people say. The advantage of this is that you can play it back later and listen to what has been said a number of times.

Try to ask questions which encourage people to talk. You can do this by using phrases like these:
- Tell me more about…
- I am interested in…
- What happened when…?
- Can you tell us how…?
- What thoughts do you have about…?
- Can you tell us all about…?
- What else can you say about...?
- We'd like you to explain what you know about…

You may need to ask direct questions like these:
- How old are you?
- When did this happen?
- Where were you when it happened?
- Can you give three reasons…?

Practising interviews

Before you interview someone, practise your techniques.
Work in pairs or small groups. One has the role of the
interviewer. Role-play the interview with a friend pretending
to be someone you are interviewing. Then get together as
a class and watch several role-plays. Make a list of the
questions that helped the person being interviewed to
talk and provide useful information. You can use these
when you carry out the real interview.

Hot seating

**Hot seating is a game in which one
volunteer plays the role of someone
being interviewed.**

Everyone else asks questions. You might decide to put
the troll from 'The Three Billy Goats Gruff' in the hot seat.
You could find out information – but also ask about the
troll's feelings and motives. You might start by saying:
'Tell us what happened.' Then you could go on to ask:
• Why did you let the baby goat go past?
• Why didn't you want them to cross the bridge?

You could also ask general questions, such as:
• Have you always lived under the bridge?
• What would you like to do as a job?
• Are you married?
• What does your wife think about your behaviour?

Agony aunts

Lots of characters in stories might welcome advice from an agony aunt – someone who gives advice about problems.

Who might benefit from a visit to an agony aunt?
Who needs advice?
- The goats who cannot cross the bridge.
- The troll who is always being woken by the goats.
- The pigs that have been attacked by the wolf.
- Three bears whose house has been broken into.
- The woman with an enormous beanstalk in her garden.
- The giant whose house has been robbed by Jack.
- Little Miss Muffet who has a large spider in her house.
- The girl who is mistreated by three ugly sisters.

Work in pairs. One person takes the role of agony aunt and gives advice. The other is in role as a story character and asks for help with various problems. Some characters might have several different problems, for example, Cinderella.

Cinderella's problems
- Mistreated by ugly sisters.
- Needs to make friends with sisters.
- Has no mother and father doesn't help her.
- Needs to keep floors clean.
- Needs to make sure dishes are washed up.

Making a broadcast

Being a journalist is great fun. You can go one step further and make a radio broadcast or use a video or digital camera to make a short report or news programme.

Programme ideas

You could broadcast a report on:

- Children's lives in Viking, Egyptian or Greek times
- How to look after the local area
- The life of a famous person
- Caring for a pet hamster
- A class trip
- Information about tornadoes
- News about giant pandas

Other ideas for broadcasts

- Favourite poems set to simple music
- Poems by one author
- Story poems
- A dramatized story with people reading different parts
- A short play
- Songs or a collection of rhymes
- Tongue twisters and riddles
- A joke collection

Broadcasting a story

Building up a story in different ways and presenting your programme to other classes or schools or at an end of term parents' evening can be very satisfying.

Imagine you're going to build a story around a dramatic incident. The queen's necklace has been stolen. Using an interactive whiteboard, a scanner, a digital camera and a computer you could present this as a story in the following way.

News bulletin: Queen's necklace stolen

Interview with maid who last saw the necklace on a window ledge

Interview with detective who lists clues

Interview with member of local bird watching society about magpie's behaviour

News bulletin: necklace found in bird's nest

Final image: Queen thanking those involved

The sequence could be developed by adding illustrations and a voice-over telling the story. In this way you can produce a story involving pictures, photographs, video clips, interviews, news bulletins and music.

6
Drama games

Everyone likes watching TV. It's nearly all acting – and drama can be fun. Try these warm-up games to put you in the mood.

Counting game

Everyone sits in a circle. Someone is chosen to start counting. This person says 'one'. Someone else, randomly, says 'two' and so on. Everyone has to say a number at some point, but not in order round the circle. If two people say a number at the same time they are both out.

Mirror moves

Everyone sits down in pairs facing their partner. One person is the mirror. The lead person begins to make movements and the mirror has to follow the movements exactly. Try doing this while speaking slowly. Can the mirror guess which words will come next?

Giants, goblins and witches

This is a lively variation of the old game scissors, stone and paper. Split the class into two. The two groups stand at either end of the hall. Everyone decides whether to be a giant, a witch or a goblin. Giants stand tall, witches crouch and goblins crawl. The two groups walk towards each other until the teacher says a magic word, e.g. 'Abrica'. Then everyone adopts their position – tall, crouching or crawling.

- Goblins defeat giants
- Giants defeat witches
- Witches defeat goblins

Defeated children lie on the floor. The winning group is the one with the most people left standing.

Key game

To play this game you need a key, a piece of chain or some other noisy object. Everyone sits in a circle and one player sits in the centre blindfolded. Another player creeps up to the person in the middle to steal the key. The blindfolded person has to listen very carefully and then try to point directly at the thief. If they miss, the other player takes their place in the centre.

Line game

Two teams line up with equal numbers in each line. The teacher hands a card to number one in each team. On it is written a category. At the word 'go' each child in turn says a word that fits into the category, or sits down. The winning team is the one which finishes first with the fewest sitting down. Categories might include cars, toys, TV programmes, pop groups, names, fruit, vegetables, etc.

Mime it

Try miming a hobby or sport and see whether others can guess what you are doing. Another idea is to pretend that you are moulding the air into a shape, rather like a potter making a pot out of air. Try to make it obvious what you are moulding by exaggerating the shape.

Thoughts in the head

Someone is chosen to role-play a character from a story the class is reading. They have to think aloud the character's thoughts and everyone else must guess who they are. This game works best if you choose an exciting moment or a point in a story when the character has a big decision to make or lots to think about.

Phone calls

Work in pairs to play this game. One of you is in role as a character from a story. The other is a friend or relative. The story character pretends to phone a friend and tells them what has been happening – and what might happen next. The friend is allowed to ask questions.

Improvisation

Improvisation is a simple idea – it's just pretend play really. There are different ways into doing this. Try some of these as starting points.

• Build an improvisation around a given word that has to be used, e.g. mouse.
• Choose a character or setting from a list and become the character in the setting.
• Select an object to use in the improvisation.

Putting on a play

One of the easiest ways to begin is to take a well-known story such as 'The Three Bears' and create your own version.

Work together to decide how many scenes you need. Think about the number of actors. Remember you will need costumes as well as scenery to make the play realistic. You may want to add songs, music and dances.

How to write a play

This is how to set out a play. The name of the person speaking is written on the left hand side and what they say on the right hand side. Stage directions are in brackets.

Big Bear   Somebody's been eating my porridge!

Mother Bear   Somebody's been eating my porridge!

Baby Bear   Somebody's been eating my porridge and they've eaten it all up! *(begins to cry)*

Tips for a successful play

All the actors need to learn their lines and be word perfect. Learning lines is easier in pairs than on your own, or you could record them on a tape and listen to the tape a lot. You also need to rehearse the play many times so that everyone knows their part and the events are clear to the audience.

Speak loudly

Speaking loudly and clearly is very important, and so is trying not to rush and gabble lines. Everyone needs to think about what their lines mean and to try to say them with the right expression. If you are saying something angry, you need to sound really cross and to show anger in your expression and gestures.

Move in character

When the actors move about on the stage, they should always try to move in the way their character would move. Think about how the character feels and move in the right way. If you are playing someone who is angry, you can stamp across the stage, but if you are playing someone who is frightened, you might creep quietly around.

Face the audience

All the actors must face the audience when they are speaking. If actors speak when they have their backs to the audience, no one will be able to hear what they say, and the audience will not be able to follow what's happening.

Have costumes and props

Dressing up helps the actors to feel like someone else and will make their performance stronger. You may need to find items for costumes at home. You will probably need some props for the play, too. These objects make the action of the play more realistic, and they can include furniture.

7
Storytelling

Everybody loves a good story. Years ago, before there were books, storytellers travelled around the country telling tales.

In the evenings, the villagers would gather round their fires to listen to stories. It was a way of life. Today, we gather round the TV – though some would say that this is not quite the same as listening to a really well told story. So how do you become a good storyteller?

Traditional tales

You can begin by retelling a well-known story, such as a traditional tale. First, find a good story that you like – it is best to start with something simple that you already know, such as 'Little Red Riding Hood'. It helps if the story has a simple pattern with some repetition – this makes learning it easier.

Now, draw a story map or storyboard showing the main characters and setting of the story (see page 50). This will help you to remember the sequence of events and also help you to see the story in your head.

Little Red Riding Hood

Use the story map to practise retelling the story.
Choose connectives from the connectives bank below to
help you link the story together. You can learn the story by
recording yourself telling it. Keep replaying your recording,
joining in with the words. Then find someone to tell it to!

Openings Once upon a time... Once (not twice)
but once upon a time... Our story begins when...

Build up One day... Early one morning... Late one
night... It happened that... So... Next... Then....

Problems Suddenly... Just then... At that moment...
Out of the blue... Unexpectedly... Unfortunately...
Without warning...

Resolution So... When... While... Whenever...
Later on... After that... Before... As... As soon as...
Immediately... Although... Because...

Endings Finally... Eventually... In the end...
So it was...

Storytelling tips

Here are a few things to remember when you are telling a story.

Begin by settling down the audience so they are ready to listen. In Armenia they say you need three ingredients – a storyteller, a story and a listener! To help the audience listen, you could begin by singing a song together, playing an instrument or chanting a rhyme.

Here are some other points to think about.
- **Volume:** make sure every one can hear.
- **Clarity:** say the words clearly.
- **Speed:** do not gabble or say the words too slowly.
- **Eyes:** look around at your audience and into their eyes!
- **Gestures:** use gestures to describe what is happening.
- **Tone:** vary your tone of voice to put expression into what you are saying.

Changing stories
Once you have learned a story, you could make it more your own by changing some parts.

You could change the names and types of character in the story. So you could retell 'The Three Billy Goats Gruff' as a story about three snowmen who want to cross the road to get into the next-door neighbour's freezer! Or you could make the wolf in 'The Three Little Pigs' a friendly character set against three mean pigs.

Try changing your story by placing it in a new setting. The gingerbread man could live in your area and you could name real places. Goldilocks could break into a department store in a nearby town. Little Red Riding Hood might live on the estate.

Traditional tales are all set a long time ago. It can be fun to change the time so they take place today. So Little Red Riding Hood might be setting off to the supermarket to buy some flapjacks for Granny.

You can add new events and scenes to the story if you want to. For example, the goats might visit the police station to complain about the bad behaviour of the troll!

Inventing new stories

Everybody likes making up new stories. There are many different ways to make up a story. See if these story banks help you.

First you need to choose a good character to be the main character in your story. Then you may want to add a bad character. Next select a setting where the story will start. Then choose a scary setting where the two characters meet. Draw a story map to help work out what will happen. A list of possible problems may be helpful too. If you get stuck, have a look at the list of possible story problems on page 56. These could help you plan your story.

Characters

Good characters

boy

girl

prince

cat

princess

woodcutter

unicorn

fisherman

Bad characters

king

queen

robber

pirate

goblin

snake

tiger

Story settings

Choose a setting for your story – it could take place in a market, a cottage, a road, a beach hut, a palace or even a tree.

Look at the drawings on these pages for ideas – or think of your own places for settings.

Tower

Market

Alleyway

Road

Beach hut

Cave

Next think about a scary setting for the story's problem or event. How about a forest, an alleyway, a lake, an old bridge, a tower, or a cave? Perhaps you can think of somewhere that you could make sound even more scary.

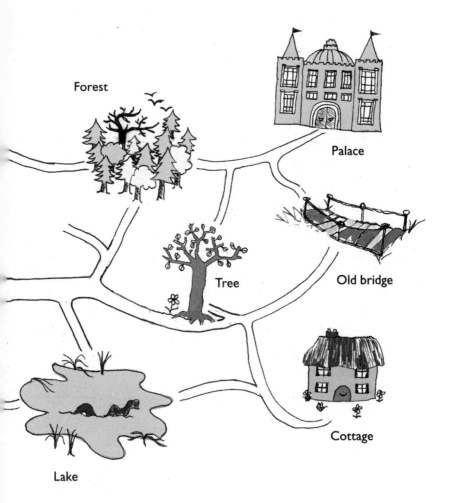

Forest

Palace

Old bridge

Tree

Cottage

Lake

The story problem

The main thing you need to make your story exciting is a problem – something that goes wrong.

The problem could be:
- A dilemma for the main character.
- Something that goes wrong.
- A frightening event.
- A scare.
- A surprise.
- A mystery to solve.

The problem lies at the heart of the story. Choose your characters and then ask yourself – what are they doing and what could go wrong?

Here are some ideas for possible problems:
- Someone tries to steal something.
- Someone gets lost.
- Someone loses something precious.
- Someone is kidnapped!
- A character is greedy.
- A monster appears.
- Someone is attacked on a journey.
- The characters visit a dangerous place.
- Someone is rescued.
- The characters go somewhere forbidden.
- The characters are chased.
- Someone loses all their money.
- Someone is chased by an evil character.

8

Performing poetry

Poetry can be performed on your own, in a pair or group, or as a class. First find a poem you enjoy that sounds good when performed.

Good poems for performance may have these features:
- A good rhythm.
- A rhyming pattern.
- Choruses.
- Places where the audience can join in.
- Repetition.
- They tell a story.
- They create a dramatic or amusing effect.

When you have found the right poem, learn it line by line until everyone can say it together. It is important that everyone listens to everyone else so that they all use the same rhythm.

Volume
Make sure that you are speaking loud enough and can be heard easily by everyone listening.

Speed
Do not chant the poem too quickly or no one will be able to understand what you are saying.

Clarity
Make sure you say the words very clearly. This may mean pronouncing the words more carefully than in normal speech.

Expression
Think about what the words mean and vary your expression so that it underlines the meaning of what you are saying.

Variation
Vary the way you say the poem. Vary the volume so some places are loud and some are soft. A clear whisper can be effective. Also, vary the speed so some of the poem is rhythmic and some is spoken quickly. Where you need to, slow down to emphasize a point. Build in pauses to add dramatic effect.

Video or tape yourselves practising. Listen to this and think about how you could improve the performance. Take it in turns to stand at the back of the room to see what the group sounds like. Do you need to be louder, clearer or to use more expression?

Extra performance ideas

To make the performance more interesting you might want to add some extras.

Here are some ideas to try:
- Add a simple but rhythmic clapping pattern to act as a beat behind the spoken performance.
- Use percussion instruments or a few chime bars to add a simple rhythm and melody.
- Dress in costumes.
- Paint and show posters to illustrate scenes.
- Put a storyboard on the interactive whiteboard and use this as a background to illustrate the performance.
- Chant the poem over a piece of quiet music that fits with the meaning of the poem.
- Display the chorus on a board or poster so that the audience can join in.
- If the poem has dialogue use actors to represent the characters.
- Add simple actions so the audience can join in.

How well did I do?

Try this quiz to check your speaking and listening skills. Write down the letter of the answer which applies best to you.

When I give a talk, my teacher says:
a) 'Try to speak a bit more slowly next time.'
b) 'Could you speak up – we can't hear you at the back.'
c) 'That was a very clear talk.'

If I was speaking in an assembly, I would:
a) Write down every word so I can stand and read it.
b) Forget about it, then say whatever comes into my head.
c) Plan what to say then practise a lot to make sure I say the right things at the right time.

During a talk, I:
a) Add in a few jokes if people start to look bored.
b) Look at my shoes so I won't get distracted.
c) Try to look round the audience while I'm speaking.

When I work in a group, I:
a) Always want to be in charge of what we do.
b) Usually forget what we're supposed to be doing and start daydreaming.
c) Take turns to speak, and always listen to what the others say.

When someone argues against me, I:
a) Shout them down.
b) Switch off and think of something else.
c) Listen to what they're saying, then reply.

In a class discussion, I:
a) Make sure everyone knows I'm right.
b) Slump in my seat so no one will ask me to speak.
c) Remember that other people may have a different view.

When someone else is talking, I:
a) Start chatting to my mates.
b) Go off into a daydream.
c) Listen, look at them and respond.

When someone gives us information, I:
a) Listen for a few moments but then get restless.
b) Decide I won't be able to remember it and switch off.
c) Remember the main points and ask questions.

Mostly As: You sound a bit over-confident. Slow down and try listening to other people before you say what you think.

Mostly Bs: Sounds as though your confidence needs a boost – and your concentration. Try listening to others and then join in. You may surprise yourself!

Mostly Cs: Sounds as though you have a good, balanced approach – well done!

Glossary

alliteration Starting words with the same sound.

audience People who are listening.

expression Changing how you say something to show your feelings, e.g. speaking in an angry voice.

group leader Someone chosen to run a group.

hot seating Someone pretending to be a character and being interviewed by the rest of the class.

improvisation Making up something on the spur of the moment.

interviewing Asking someone questions.

mentor A group member who helps to complete a task, making sure everyone has spoken and checking that everyone agrees.

mime To pretend to do something using actions, not speech.

newsreader A person on radio or television who reads the news.

pace The speed at which you talk.

persuasive language Using words to try to make someone believe what you are saying.

reporter A person whose job it is to find out news and report it for radio, television or a newspaper.

role-play Making up a scene in which everyone takes on a different role and pretends to be someone else.

scribe A person in a group who writes down the main points.

setting The place where a story happens.

storyboard A cartoon version of a story that shows the main events.

Index